ISBN 978-1-330-25590-2
PIBN 10003143

Forgotten Books is a registered trademark of FB &c Ltd.
Copyright © 2015 FB &c Ltd.
FB &c Ltd, Dalton House, 60 Windsor Avenue, London, SW19 2RR.
Company number 08720141. Registered in England and Wales.

For support please visit www.forgottenbooks.com

1 MONTH OF
FREE
READING

at
www.ForgottenBooks.com

By purchasing this book you are eligible for one month membership to ForgottenBooks.com, giving you unlimited access to our entire collection of over 700,000 titles via our web site and mobile apps.

To claim your free month visit:
www.forgottenbooks.com/free3143

Similar Books Are Available from
www.forgottenbooks.com

MR. DARWIN'S CRITICS.

1. *Contributions to the Theory of Natural Selection.* By
   A. R. WALLACE. 1870.
2. *The Genesis of Species.* By ST. G. MIVART, F.R.S.
   Second Edition. 1871.
3. *Darwin's Descent of Man.* Quarterly Review. July,
   1871.

THE gradual lapse of time has now separated us by more than a decade from the date of the publication of the "Origin of Species"—and whatever may be thought or said about Mr. Darwin's doctrines, or the manner in which he has propounded them, this much is certain, that, in a dozen years, the "Origin of Species" has worked as complete a revolution in biological science as the "Principia" did in astronomy—and it has done so, because, in the words of Helmholtz, it contains "an essentially new creative thought."*

And as time has slipped by, a happy change has come over Mr. Darwin's critics. The mixture of ignorance and insolence which, at first, characterised a large proportion of the attacks with which he was assailed, is no longer the sad distinction of anti-Darwinian criticism. Instead of abusive nonsense, which merely discredited its writers, we read essays, which are, at worst, more or less intelligent and appreciative; while, sometimes, like that which appeared in the *North British Review* for 1867, they have a real and permanent value.

The several publications of Mr. Wallace and Mr. Mivart contain discussions of some of Mr. Darwin's views, which are worthy of particular attention, not only on account of the acknowledged scientific competence of these writers, but because they exhibit an attention to

* Helmholtz: Ueber das Ziel und die Fortschritte der Naturwissenchaft. Eröffnungsrede für die Naturforscherversammlung zu Innsbruck. 1869.

those philosophical questions which underlie all physical science, which is as rare as it is needful. And the same may be said of an article in the *Quarterly Review* for July 1871, the comparison of which with an article in the same Review for July, 1860, is perhaps the best evidence which can be brought forward of the change which has taken place in public opinion on " Darwinism."

The Quarterly Reviewer admits " the certainty of the action of natural selection " (p. 49); and further allows that there is an *à priori* probability in favour of the evolution of man from some lower animal form, if these lower animal forms themselves have arisen by evolution.

Mr. Wallace and Mr. Mivart go much further than this. They are as stout believers in evolution as Mr. Darwin himself; but Mr. Wallace denies that man can have been evolved from a lower animal by that process of natural selection which he, with Mr. Darwin, holds to have been sufficient for the evolution of all animals below man ; while Mr. Mivart, admitting that natural selection has been one of the conditions of the evolution of the animals below man, maintains that natural selection must, even in their case, have been supplemented by " some other cause "—of the nature of which, unfortunately, he does not give us any idea. Thus Mr. Mivart is less of a Darwinian than Mr. Wallace, for he has less faith in the power of natural selection. But he is more of an evolutionist than Mr. Wallace, because Mr. Wallace thinks it necessary to call in an intelligent agent —a sort of supernatural Sir John Sebright—to produce even the animal frame of man ; while Mr. Mivart requires no Divine assistance till he comes to man's soul.

Thus there is a considerable divergence between Mr. Wallace and Mr. Mivart. On the other hand, there are some curious similarities between Mr. Mivart and the Quarterly Reviewer, and these are sometimes so close, that, if Mr. Mivart thought it worth while, I think he might make out a good case of plagiarism against the Reviewer, who studiously abstains from quoting him.

Both the Reviewer and Mr. Mivart reproach Mr. Darwin with being, " like so many other physicists," entangled in a radically false metaphysical system, and with setting at naught the first principles of both philosophy and religion. Both enlarge upon the necessity of a sound philosophical basis, and both, I venture to add, make a conspicuous exhibition of its absence. The Quarterly Reviewer believes that man " differs more from an elephant or a gorilla than do these from the dust of the earth on which they tread," and Mr. Mivart has expressed the opinion that there is more difference between man and an ape than there is between an ape and a piece of granite.*

* See the *Tablet* for March 11, 1871.

And even when Mr. Mivart trips in a matter of anatomy, and creates a difficulty for Mr. Darwin out of a supposed close similarity between the eyes of fishes and cephalopods, which (as Gegenbaur and others have clearly shown) does not exist (p. 86), the Quarterly Reviewer adopts the argument without hesitation (p. 66).

There is another important point, however, in which it is hard to say whether Mr. Mivart diverges from the Quarterly Reviewer or not.

The Reviewer declares that Mr. Darwin has, "with needless opposition, set at nought the first principles of both philosophy and religion" (p. 90).

It looks, at first, as if this meant, that Mr. Darwin's views being false, the opposition to "religion" which flows from them must be needless. But I suspect this is not the right view of the meaning of the passage, as Mr. Mivart, from whom the Quarterly Reviewer plainly draws so much inspiration, tells us that "the consequences which have been drawn from evolution, whether exclusively Darwinian or not, to the prejudice of religion, by no means follow from it, and are in fact illegitimate" (p. 5).

I may assume, then, that the Quarterly Reviewer and Mr. Mivart admit that there is no necessary opposition between "evolution, whether exclusively Darwinian or not," and religion. But then, what do they mean by this last much-abused term? On this point the Quarterly Reviewer is silent. Mr. Mivart, on the contrary, is perfectly explicit, and the whole tenor of his remarks leaves no doubt that by "religion" he means theology; and by theology, that particular variety of the great Proteus, which is expounded by the doctors of the Roman Catholic Church, and held by the members of that religious community to be the sole form of absolute truth and of saving faith.

According to Mr. Mivart, the greatest and most orthodox authorities upon matters of Catholic doctrine agree in distinctly asserting "derivative creation" or evolution; "and thus their teachings harmonize with all that modern science can possibly require" (p. 305).

I confess that this bold assertion interested me more than anything else in Mr. Mivart's book. What little knowledge I possessed of Catholic doctrine, and of the influence exerted by Catholic authority in former times, had not led me to expect that modern science was likely to find a warm welcome within the pale of the greatest and most consistent of theological organizations.

And my astonishment reached its climax when I found Mr. Mivart citing Father Suarez as his chief witness in favour of the scientific freedom enjoyed by Catholics—the popular repute of that learned theologian and subtle casuist not being such as make his works a likely place of refuge for liberality of thought. But in these days, when Judas Iscariot and Robespierre, Henry VIII., and Catiline, have all been shown to be men of admirable virtue, far in advance of their age, and consequently the victims of vulgar prejudice, it was obviously possible that Jesuit Suarez might be in like case. And, spurred by Mr. Mivart's unhesitating declaration, I hastened to acquaint myself with such of the works of the great Catholic divine as bore upon the question, hoping, not merely to acquaint myself with the true teachings of the infallible Church, and free myself of an unjust prejudice; but, haply, to enable myself, at a pinch, to put some Protestant bibliolater to shame, by the bright example of Catholic freedom from the trammels of verbal inspiration.

I regret to say that my anticipations have been cruelly disappointed. But the extent to which my hopes have been crushed can only be fully appreciated by citing, in the first place, those passages of Mr. Mivart's work by which they were excited. In his introductory chapter I find the following passages :—

"The prevalence of this theory [of evolution] need alarm no one, for it is, without any doubt, perfectly consistent with the strictest and most orthodox Christian* theology " (p. 5).

"Mr. Darwin and others may perhaps be excused if they have not devoted much time to the study of Christian philosophy; but they have no right to assume or accept, without careful examination, as an unquestioned fact, that in that philosophy there is a necessary antagonism between the two ideas 'creation' and 'evolution,' as applied to organic forms.

"It is notorious and patent to all who choose to seek, that many distinguished Christian thinkers have accepted, and do accept, both ideas, *i.e.*, both ' creation' and 'evolution.'

"As much as ten years ago an eminently Christian writer observed: 'The creationist theory does not necessitate the perpetual search after manifestations of miraculous power and perpetual " catastrophes." Creation is not a miraculous interference with the laws of nature, but the very institution of those laws. Law and regularity, not arbitrary intervention, was the patristic ideal of creation. With this notion they admitted, without difficulty, the most surprising origin of living creatures, provided it took place by *law*. They held that when God said, " Let the waters produce," " Let the earth produce," He conferred forces on the elements of earth and water, which enabled them naturally to produce the various species of organic beings. This power, they thought, remains attached to the elements throughout all time.' The same writer quotes St.

---

* It should be observed that Mr. Mivart employs the term " Christian " as if it were the equivalent of " Catholic."

Augustin and St. Thomas Aquinas, to the effect that, 'in the institution of nature, we do not look for miracles, but for the laws of nature.' And, again, St. Basil speaks of the continued operation of natural laws in the production of all organisms.

" So much for the writers of early and mediæval times. As to the present day, the author can confidently affirm that there are many as well versed in theology as Mr. Darwin is in his own department of natural knowledge, who would not be disturbed by the thorough demonstration of his theory. Nay, they would not even be in the least painfully affected at witnessing the generation of animals of complex organization by the skilful artificial arrangement of natural forces, and the production, in the future, of a fish by means analogous to those by which we now produce urea.

" And this because they know that the possibility of such phenomena, though by no means actually foreseen, has yet been fully provided for in the old philosophy centuries before Darwin, or even centuries before Bacon, and that their place in the system can be at once assigned them without even disturbing its order or marring its harmony.

" Moreover, the old tradition in this respect has never been abandoned, however much it may have been ignored or neglected by some modern writers. In proof of this, it may be observed that perhaps no post-mediæval theologian has a wider reception amongst Christians throughout the world than Suarez, who has a separate section * in opposition to those who maintain the distinct creation of the various kinds—or substantial forms—of organic life " (pp. 19—21).

Still more distinctly does Mr. Mivart express himself, in the same sense, in his last chapter, entitled " Theology and Evolution " (pp. 302—5).

" It appears, then, that Christian thinkers are perfectly free to accept the general evolution theory. But are there any theological authorities to justify this view of the matter ?

" Now, considering how extremely recent are these biological speculations, it might hardly be expected à priori that writers of earlier ages should have given expression to doctrines harmonizing in any degree with such very modern views; nevertheless, this is certainly the case, and it would be easy to give numerous examples. It will be better, however, to cite one or two authorities of weight. Perhaps no writer of the earlier Christian ages could be quoted whose authority is more generally recognised than that of St. Augustin. The same may be said of the mediæval period for St. Thomas Aquinas: and since the movement of Luther, Suarez may

---

* Suarez, Metaphysica. Edition Vivés. Paris, 1868, vol. i. Disputat, xv. § 2.

be taken as an authority, widely venerated, and one whose orthodoxy has never been questioned.

"It must be borne in mind that for a considerable time even after the last of these writers no one had disputed the generally received belief as to the small age of the world, or at least of the kinds of animals and plants inhabiting it. It becomes, therefore, much more striking if views formed under such a condition of opinion are found to harmonize with modern ideas concerning 'Creation' and organic Life.

"Now St. Augustin insists in a very remarkable manner on the merely derivative sense in which God's creation of organic forms is to be understood; that is, that God created them by conferring on the material world the power to evolve them under suitable conditions."

Mr. Mivart then cites certain passages from St. Augustin, St. Thomas Aquinas, and Cornelius à Lapide, and finally adds;—

"As to Suarez, it will be enough to refer to Disp. xv. sec. 2, No. 9, p. 508, t. i. edition Vivés, Paris; also No. 13—15. Many other references to the same effect could easily be given, but these may suffice.

"It is then evident that ancient and most venerable theological authorities distinctly assert *derivative* creation, and thus their teachings harmonize with all that modern science can possibly require."

It will be observed that Mr. Mivart refers solely to Suarez's fifteenth Disputation, though he adds, "Many other references to the same effect could easily be given." I shall look anxiously for these references in the third edition of the "Genesis of Species." For the present, all I can say is, that I have sought in vain, either in the fifteenth Disputation, or elsewhere, for any passage in Suarez's writings which, in the slightest degree, bears out Mr. Mivart's views as to his opinions.*

The title of this fifteenth Disputation is "De causa formali substantiali," and the second section of that Disputation (to which Mr. Mivart refers) is headed, "Quomodo possit forma substantialis fieri in materia et ex materia?"

The problem which Suarez discusses in this place may be popularly stated thus: According to the scholastic philosophy every natural body has two components—the one its "matter" (*materia prima*), the other its "substantial form" (*forma substantialis*). Of these the matter is everywhere the same, the matter of one body being indistinguishable from the matter of any other body. That which differentiates any one natural body from all others is its substantial form, which inheres in the matter of that body, as the

---

* The edition of Suarez's "Disputationes" from which the following citations are given, is Birckmann's, in two volumes folio, and is dated 1630.

human soul inheres in the matter of the frame of man, and is the source of all the activities and other properties of the body.

Thus, says Suarez, if water is heated, and the source of heat is then removed, it cools again. The reason of this is that there is a certain *"intimius principium"* in the water, which brings it back to the cool condition when the external impediment to the existence of that condition is removed. This *intimius principium* is the "substantial form" of the water. And the substantial form of the water is not only the cause (*radix*) of the coolness of the water, but also of its moisture, of its density, and of all its other properties.

It will thus be seen that "substantial forms" play nearly the same part in the scholastic philosophy as "forces" do in modern science; the general tendency of modern thought being to conceive all bodies as resolvable into material particles and forces, in virtue of which last, these particles assume those dispositions and exercise those powers which are characteristic of each particular kind of matter.

But the schoolmen distinguished two kinds of substantial forms, the one spiritual and the other material. The former division is represented by the human soul, the *anima rationalis*; and they affirm as a matter, not merely of reason, but of faith, that every human soul is created out of nothing, and by this act of creation is endowed with the power of existing for all eternity, apart from the *materia prima* of which the corporeal frame of man is composed. And the *anima rationalis*, once united with the *materia prima* of the body, becomes its substantial form, and is the source of all the powers and faculties of man—of all the vital and sensitive phenomena which he exhibits—just as the substantial form of water is the source of all its qualities.

The "material substantial forms" are those which inform all other natural bodies except that of man; and the object of Suarez in the present Disputation, is to show that the axiom "*ex nihilo nihil fit*," though not true of the substantial form of man, is true of the substantial forms of all other bodies, the endless mutations of which constitute the ordinary course of nature. The origin of the difficulty which he discusses is easily comprehensible. Suppose a piece of bright iron to be exposed to the air. The existence of the iron depends on the presence within it of a substantial form, which is the cause of its properties, *e.g.*, brightness, hardness, weight. But, by degrees, the iron becomes converted into a mass of rust, which is dull, and soft, and light, and, in all other respects, is quite different from the iron. As, in the scholastic view, this difference is due to the rust being informed by a new substantial form, the grave problem arises, how did this new substantial form come into being? Has it been created? or has it arisen by the power of natural causation? If the former hypothesis is correct, then the axiom, "*ex nihilo nihil fit*," is false, even in relation to the ordinary course of nature, seeing that such mutations of matter as imply the continual origin of new substantial forms are occurring every moment. But the harmonization of Aristotle with theology was as dear to the schoolmen, as the smoothing down the differences between Moses and science is to our Broad Churchmen, and they were proportionably unwilling to contradict one of Aristotle's fundamental propositions. Nor was their objection to flying in the face of the Stagirite likely to be lessened by the fact that such flight landed them in flat Pantheism.

So Father Suarez fights stoutly for the second hypothesis; and I quote the principal part of his argumentation as an exquisite specimen of that speech which is a " darkening of counsel."

"13. Secundo de omnibus aliis formis substantialibus [sc. materialibus] dicendum est non fieri proprie ex nihilo, sed ex potentia præjacentis materiæ educi : ideoque in effectione harum formarum nil fieri contra illud axioma, *Ex nihilo nihil fit,* si recte intelligatur. Hæc assertio sumitur ex Aristotele 1. Physicorum per totum et libro 7. Metaphyss. et ex aliis authoribus, quos statim referam. Et declaratur breviter, nam fieri ex nihilo duo dicit, unum est fieri absolute et simpliciter, aliud est quod talis effectio fit ex nihilo. Primum proprie dicitur de re subsistente, quia ejus est fieri, cujus est esse : id autem proprie quod subsistit et habet esse ; nam quod alteri adjacet, potius est quo aliud est. Ex hac ergo parte, formæ substantiales materiales non fiunt ex nihilo, quia proprie non fiunt. Atque hanc rationem reddit Divus Thomas 1. parte, quæstione 45, articulo 8. et quæstione 90. articulo 2. et ex dicendis magis explicabitur. Sumendo ergo ipsum *fieri* in hac proprietate et rigore, sic fieri ex nihilo est fieri secundum se totum, id est nulla sui parte præsupposita, ex qua fiat. Et hac ratione res naturales dum de novo fiunt, non fiunt ex nihilo,' quia fiunt ex præsupposita materia, ex qua componuntur, et ita non fiunt, secundum se totæ, sed secundum aliquid sui. Formæ autem harum rerum, quamvis revera totam suam entitatem de novo accipiant, quam antea non habebant, quia vero ipsæ non fiunt, ut dictum est, ideo neque ex nihilo fiunt. Attamen, quia latiori modo sumendo verbum illud *fieri,* negari non potest : quin forma facta sit, eo modo quo nunc est, et antea non erat, ut etiam probat ratio dubitandi posita in principio sectionis, ideo addendum est, sumpto *fieri* in hac amplitudine, fieri ex nihilo non tameu negare habitudinem materialis causæ intrinsece componentis id quod fit, sed etiam habitudinem causæ materialis per se causantis et sustentantis formam quæ fit, seu confit. Diximus enim in superioribus materiam et esse causam compositi et formæ dependentis ab illa : ut res ergo dicatur ex nihilo fieri uterque modus causalitatis negari debet ; et eodem sensu accipiendium est illud axioma, ut sit verum : *Ex nihilo nihil fit,* scilicet virtute agentis naturalis et finiti nihil fieri, nisi ex præsupposito subjecto per se concurrente, et ad compositum et ad formam, si utrumque suo modo ab eodem agente fiat. Ex his ergo recte concluditur, formas substantiales materiales non fieri ex nihilo, quia fiunt ex materia, quæ in suo genere per se concurrit, et influit ad esse, et fieri talium formarum ; quia, sicut esse non possunt nisi affixæ materiæ, à qua sustententur in esse : ita nec fieri possunt, nisi earum effectio et penetratio in eadem materia sustentetur. Et hæc est propria et per se differentia inter effectionem ex nihilo, et ex aliquo, propter quam, ut infra ostendemus, prior modus efficiendi superat vim finitam naturalium agentium, non vero posterior.

"14. Ex his etiam constat, proprie de his formis dici ·non creari, sed educi de potentia materiæ." *

If I may venture to interpret these hard sayings, Suarez conceives that the evolution of substantial forms in the ordinary course of nature, is conditioned not only by the existence of the *materia prima*, but also by a certain "concurrence and influence" which that *materia* exerts; and every new substantial form being thus conditioned, and in part, at any rate, caused, by a pre-existing something, cannot be said to be created out of nothing.

But as the whole tenor of the context shows, Suarez applies this argumentation merely to the evolution of material substantial forms in the ordinary course of nature. How the substantial forms of animals and plants primarily originated, is a question to which, so far as I am able to discover, he does not so much as allude in his "Metaphysical Disputations." Nor was there any necessity that he should do so, inasmuch as he has devoted a separate treatise of considerable bulk to the discussion of all the problems which arise out of the account of the creation which is given in the Book of Genesis. And it is a matter of wonderment to me that Mr. Mivart, who somewhat sharply reproves "Mr. Darwin and others" for not acquainting themselves with the true teachings of his Church, should allow himself to be indebted to a heretic like myself for a knowledge of the existence of that "Tractatus de opere sex dierum," † in which the learned Father, of whom he justly speaks, as "an authority widely venerated, and whose orthodoxy has never been questioned," directly opposes all those opinions, for which Mr. Mivart claims the shelter of his authority.

In the tenth and eleventh chapters of the first book of this treatise, Suarez inquires in what sense the word "day," as employed in the first chapter of Genesis, is to be taken. He discusses the views of Philo and of Augustin on this question, and rejects them. He suggests that the approval of their allegorising interpretations by St. Thomas Aquinas, merely arose out of St. Thomas's modesty, and his desire not to seem openly to controvert St. Augustin—" voluisse Divus Thomas pro sua modestia subterfugere vim argumenti potins quam aperte Augustinum inconstantiæ arguere."

Finally, Suarez decides that the writer of Genesis meant that the term "day" should be taken in its natural sense; and he winds up the discussion with the very just and natural remark that "it is not probable that God, in inspiring Moses to write a history of the

* Suarez, *l. c.* Dispu., xv. § 11.

† Tractatus de opere sex Dierum, seu de Universi Creatione, quatenus sex diebus perfecta esse, in libro Genesis cap. i. refertur, et præsertim de productione hominis in statu innocentiæ. Ed. Birckmann. 1622.

Creation which was to be believed by ordinary people, would have made him use language, the true meaning of which it is hard to discover, and still harder to believe." *

And in chapter xii. 3, Suarez further observes:—

" Ratio enim retinendi veram significationem diei naturalis est illa communis, quod verba Scripturæ non sunt ad metaphoras transferenda, nisi vel necessitas cogit, vel ex ipsa scriptura constet, et maximè in historica narratione et ad instructionem fidei pertinente : sed hæc ratio non minus cogit ad intelligendum propriè dierum numerum, quam diei qualitatem, QUIA NON MINUS UNO MODO QUAM ALIO DESTRUITUR SINCERITAS, IMO ET VERITAS HISTORIÆ. Secundo hoc valde confirmant alia Scripturæ loca, in quibus hi sex dies tanquam veri, et inter se distincti commemorantur, ut Exod. 20 dicitur, *Sex diebus operabis et facies omnia opera tua, septimo autem die Sabbatum Domini Dei tui.est.* Et infra : *Sex enim diebus fecit Dominus cælum et terram et mare et omnia quæ in eis sunt,* et idem repetitur in cap. 31. In quibus locis sermonis proprietas colligi potest tum ex æquiparatione, nam cum dicitur : *sex diebus operabis,* propreissimè intelligitur : tum quia non est verisimile, potuisse populum intelligere verba illa in alio sensu, et è contrario incredibile est, Deum in suis præceptis tradendis illis verbis ad populum fuisse loquutum, quibus deciperetur, falsum sensum concipiendo, si Deus non per sex veros dies opera sua fecisset."

*T*hese passages leave no doubt that this great doctor of the Catholic Church, of unchallenged authority and unspotted orthodoxy, not only declares it to be Catholic doctrine that the work of creation took place in the space of six natural days; but that he warmly repudiates, as inconsistent with our knowledge of the divine attributes, the supposition that the language which Catholic faith requires the believer to hold that God inspired, was used in any other sense than that which He knew it would convey to the minds of those to whom it was addressed.

And I think that in this repudiation Father Suarez will have the sympathy of every man of common uprightness, to whom it is certainly " incredible " that the Almighty should have acted in a manner which he would esteem dishonest and base in a man.

But the belief that the universe was created in six natural days is hopelessly inconsistent with the doctrine of evolution, in so far as it applies to the stars and planetary bodies ; and it can be made to agree with a belief in the evolution of living beings only by the supposition that the plants and animals, which are said to have been created on the third, fifth, and six days, were merely the primordial forms, or rudiments, out of which existing plants and animals have been evolved; so that, on these days, plants and animals were not created actually, but only potentially.

---

* " Propter hæc ergo sententia illa Augustini et propter nimiam obscuritatem et subtilitatem ejus difficilis creditu est : quia verisimile non est Deum inspirasse Moysi, ut historiam de creatione mundi ad fidem totius populi adeò necessariam per nomina dierum explicaret, quorum significatio vix inveniri et difficillime ab aliquo credi posset." (*l. c.* Lib. I. cap. xi. 42).

The latter view is that held by Mr. Mivart, who follows St. Augustin, and implies that he has the sanction of Suarez. But, in point of fact, the latter great light of orthodoxy takes no small pains to give the most explicit and direct contradiction to all such imaginations, as the following passages prove. In the first place, as regards plants, Suarez discusses the problem :—

Quomodo herba virens et cætera vegetabilia hoc [*tertio*] *die fuerint producta.**

"Præcipua enim difficultas hîc est, quam attingit Div. Thomas 1, par. qu. 69, art. 2, an hæc productio plantarum hoc die facta intelligenda sit de productione ipsarum in proprio esse actuali et formali (ut sic rem explicerem) vel de productione tantùm in semine et in potentia. Nam Divus Augustinus libro quinto Genes. ad liter. cap. 4 et 5 et libro 8, cap. 3, posteriorem partem tradit, dicens, terram in hoc die accepisse virtutem germinandi omnia vegetabilia quasi concepto omnium illorum semine, non tamen statim vegetabilia omnia produxisse. Quod primo suadet verbis illis capitis secundi. *In die quo fecit Deus cœlum et terram et omne virgultum agri priusquam germinaret.* Quomodo enim potuerunt virgulta fieri antequam terra germinaret, nisi quia causaliter prius et quasi in radice, seu in semine facta sunt, et postea in actu producta ? Secundò confirmari potest, quia verbum illud *germinet terra* optimè exponitur potestativè ut sic dicam, id est, accipiat terra vim germinandi. Sicut in eodem capite dicitur *cresciti et multiplicamini.* Tertio potest confirmari, quia actualis productio vegetabilium non tam ad opus creationis, quam ad opus propagationis pertinet, quod postea factum est. Et hanc sententiam sequitur Eucherius lib. 1, in Gen. cap. 11, et illi faveat Glossa, interli. Hugo. et Lyran. dum verbum *germinet* dicto modo exponunt. NIHILOMINUS CONTRARIA SENTENTIA TENENDA EST : SCILICET, PRODUXISSE DEUM HOC DIE HERBAM, ARBORES, ET ALIA VEGETABILIA ACTU IN PROPRIA SPECIE ET NATURA. Hæc est communis sententia Patrum.—Basil. homil. 5 ; Exæmer. Ambros. lib. 3 ; Exæmer. cap. 8, 11 et 16 ; Chrysost. homil. 5 in Gen. Damascene lib. 2 de Fid., cap. 10. ; Theodor. Cyrilli, Bedæ, Glossæ ordinariæ et aliorum in Gen. Et idem sentit Divus Thomas, *supra*, solvens argumenta Augustini, quamvis propter reverentiam ejus quasi problematicè semper procedat. Denique idem sentiunt omnes qui in his operibus veram successionem et temporalem distinctionem agnoscant."

Secondly, with respect to animals, Suarez is no less decided :—

" *De animalium ratione carentium productione quinto et sexto die factu.**

" 32. Primò ergo nobis certum sit hæc animantia non in virtute tantum aut in semine, sed actu, et in seipsis, facta fuisse his diebus in quibus facta narrantur. Quanquam Augustinus lib. 3, Gen ad liter. cap. 5 in sua persistens sententia contrarium sentire videatur."

But Suarez proceeds to refute Augustin's opinions at great length, and his final judgment may be gathered from the following passage :—

" 35. Tertio dicendum est, hæc animalia omnia his diebus producta esse, IN PERFECTO STATU, IN SINGULIS INDIVIDUIS, SEU SPECIEBUS SUIS, JUXTA UNIUS-CUJUSQUE NATURAM. . . . . ITAQUE FUERUNT OMNIA CREATA INTEGRA ET OMNIBUS SUIS MEMBRIS PERFECTA." . . . .

l. c. Lib. II., cap. vii. and viii. 1, 32, 35.

As regards the creation of animals and plants, therefore, it is clear that Suarez, so far from "distinctly asserting derivative creation," denies it as distinctly and positively as he can; that he is at much pains to refute St. Augustin's opinions; that he does not hesitate to regard the faint acquiescence of St. Thomas Aquinas in the views of his brother saint as a kindly subterfuge on the part of Divus Thomas; and that he affirms his own view to be that which is supported by the authority of the Fathers of the Church. So that, when Mr. Mivart tells us that "Catholic theology is in harmony with all that modern science can possibly require;" that "to the general theory of evolution, and to the special Darwinian form of it, no exception . . . need be taken on the ground of orthodoxy;" and that "law and regularity, not arbitrary intervention, was the Patristic ideal of creation," we have to choose between his dictum, as a theologian, and that of a great light of his Church, whom he himself declares to be "widely venerated as an authority, and whose orthodoxy has never been questioned."

But Mr. Mivart does not hesitate to push his attempt to harmonize science with Catholic orthodoxy to its utmost limit; and, while assuming that the soul of man "arises from immediate and direct creation," he supposes that his body was "formed at first (as now in each separate individual) by derivative, or secondary creation, through natural laws" (p. 331).

This means, I presume, that an animal, having the corporeal form and bodily powers of man, may have been developed out of some lower form of life by a process of evolution; and that, after this anthropoid animal had existed for a longer or shorter time, God made a soul by direct creation, and put it into the manlike body, which, heretofore, had been devoid of that *anima rationalis*, which is supposed to be man's distinctive character.

This hypothesis is incapable of either proof or disproof, and therefore may be true; but if Suarez is any authority it is not Catholic doctrine. "Nulla est in homine forma educta de potentia materiæ,"* is a dictum which is absolutely inconsistent with the doctrine of the natural evolution of any vital manifestation of the human body.

Moreover, if man existed as an animal before he was provided with a rational soul, he must, in accordance with the elementary requirements of the philosophy in which Mr. Mivart delights, have possessed a distinct sensitive and vegetative soul, or souls. Hence, when the "breath of life" was breathed into the manlike animal's nostrils, he must have already been a living and feeling creature. But Suarez particularly discusses this point, and not only rejects Mr. Mivart's view, but adopts language of very theological strength regarding it.

* Disput. xv. § x. No. 27.

"Possent præterea his adjungi argumenta theologica, ut est illud quod sumitur ex illis verbis Genes. 2. *Formavit Deus hominem ex limo terræ et inspiravit in faciem ejus spiraculum vitæ et factus est homo in animam viventem:* ille enim spiritus, quem Deus spiravit, anima rationalis fuit, et PER EADEM FACTUS EST HOMO VIVENS, ET CONSEQUENTER, ETIAM SENTIENS.

"Aliud est ex VIII. Synodo Generali quæ est Constantinopolitana IV. can. 11, qui sic habet. *Apparet quosdam in tantum impietatis venisse ut homines duas animas habere dogmatizent: talis igitur impietatis inventores et similes sapientes, cum vetus et novum testamentum omnesque Ecclesiæ patres unam animam rationalem hominem habere asseverent, Sancta et universalis Synodus anathematizat.*" *

Moreover, if the animal nature of man was the result of evolution, so must that of woman have been. But the Catholic doctrine, according to Suarez, is that woman was, in the strictest and most literal sense of the words, made out of the rib of man.

"Nihilominus sententia Catholica est, verba illa Scripturæ esse ad literam intelligenda. AC PROINDE VERE, AC REALITER, TULISSE DEUM COSTAM ADÆ, ET, EX ILLA, CORPUS EVÆ FORMASSE." †

Nor is there any escape in the supposition that some woman existed before Eve, after the fashion of the Lilith of the rabbis ; since Suarez qualifies that notion, along with some other Judaic imaginations, as simply "damnabilis." ‡

After the perusal of the "Tractatus de Opere" it is, in fact, impossible to admit that Suarez held any opinion respecting the origin of species except such as is consistent with the strictest and most literal interpretation of the words of Genesis. For Suarez, it is Catholic doctrine, that the world was made in six natural days. On the first of these days the *materia prima* was made out of nothing, to receive afterwards those "substantial forms" which moulded it into the universe of things ; on the third day, the ancestors of all living plants suddenly came into being, full-grown, perfect, and possessed of all the properties which now distinguish them ; while, on the fifth and sixth days, the ancestors of all existing animals were similarly caused to exist in their complete and perfect state, by the infusion of their appropriate material substantial forms into the matter which had already been created. Finally, on the sixth day, the *anima rationalis* —that rational and immortal substantial form which is peculiar to man—was created out of nothing, and "breathed into" a mass of matter which, till then, was mere dust of the earth, and so man arose. But the species man was represented by a solitary male individual, until the Creator took out one of his ribs and fashioned it into a female.

This is the view of the "Genesis of Species," held by Suarez to be

* Disput., xv., "De causa formali substantiali," § x. No. 24.
† "Tractatus de Opere," Lib. III., "De hominis creatione," cap. ii. No. 3.
‡ Ibid. Lib. III. cap. iv., Nos. 8 and 9.

the only one consistent with Catholic faith ; it is because he holds this view to be Catholic that he does not hesitate to declare St. Augustin unsound, and St. Thomas Aquinas guilty of weakness, when the one swerved from this view and the other tolerated the deviation. And, until responsible Catholic authority—say, for example, the Archbishop of Westminster—formally declares that Suarez was wrong, and that Catholic priests are free to teach their flocks that the world was *not* made in six natural days, and that plants and animals were *not* created in their perfect and complete state, but have been evolved by natural processes through long ages from certain germs in which they were potentially contained, I, for one, shall feel bound to believe that the doctrines of Suarez are the only ones which are sanctioned by Infallible Authority, as represented by the Holy Father and the Catholic Church. .

I need hardly add that they are as absolutely denied and repudiated by Scientific Authority, as represented by Reason and Fact. The question whether the earth and the immediate progenitors of its present living population were made in six natural days or not, is no longer one upon which two opinions can be held.

The fact that it did not so come into being stands upon as sound a basis as any fact of history whatever. It is not true that existing plants and animals came into being within three days of the creation of the earth out of nothing, for it is certain that innumerable generations of other plants and animals lived upon the earth before its present population. And when, Sunday after Sunday, men who profess to be our instructors in righteousness read out the statement, " In six days the Lord made heaven and earth, the sea, and all that in them is," in innumerable churches, they are either propagating what they may easily know, and, therefore, are bound to know, to be falsities ; or, if they use the words in some non-natural sense, they fall below the moral standard of the much abused Jesuit.

Thus far the contradiction between Catholic verity and Scientific verity is complete and absolute, quite independently of the truth or falsehood of the doctrine of evolution. But, for those who hold the doctrine of evolution, all the Catholic verities about the creation of living beings must be no less false. For them, the assertion that the progenitors of all existing plants were made on the third day, of animals on the fifth and sixth days, in the forms they now present, is simply false. Nor can they admit that man was made suddenly out of the dust of the earth ; while it would be an insult to ask an evolutionist whether he credits the preposterous fable respecting the fabrication of woman to which Suarez pins his faith. If Suarez has rightly stated Catholic doctrine, then is evolution utter heresy. And such I believe it to be. In addition to the truth of the doctrine of evolution, indeed, one of its greatest merits in my eyes, is the fact that it occupies a position of complete and irreconcilable antagonism to that vigorous and consistent enemy of the highest intellectual, moral, and social life of mankind—the Catholic Church. No doubt, Mr. Mivart, like other putters of new wine into old bottles, is actuated by motives which are worthy of respect, and even of sympathy; but his attempt has met with the fate which the Scripture prophesies for all such.

Catholic theology, like all theologies which are based upon the assumption of the truth of the account of the origin of things given in the book of Genesis, being utterly irreconcilable with the doctrine of evolution, the student of science, who is satisfied that the evidence upon which the doctrine of evolution rests, is incomparably stronger and better than that upon which the supposed authority of the book of Genesis rests, will not trouble himself further with these theologies, but will confine his attention to such arguments against the view he holds as are based upon purely scientific data—and by scientific data I do not merely mean the truths of physical, mathematical, or logical science, but those of moral and metaphysical science. For, by science, I understand all knowledge which rests upon evidence and reasoning of a like character to that which claims our assent to ordinary scientific propositions. And if any one is able to make good the assertion that his theology rests upon valid evidence and sound reasoning, then it appears to me that such theology will take its place as a part of science.

The present antagonism between theology and science does not arise from any assumption by the men of science that all theology must necessarily be excluded from science; but simply because they are unable to allow that reason and morality have two weights and two measures; and that the belief in a proposition, because authority tells you it is true, or because you wish to believe it, which is a high crime and misdemeanour when the subject matter of reason is of one kind, becomes under the *alias* of "faith" the greatest of all virtues, when the subject matter of reason is of another kind.

The Bishop of Brechin said well the other day:—"Liberality in religion—I do not mean tender and generous allowances for the mistakes of others—is only unfaithfulness to truth."* And, with the same qualification, I venture to paraphrase the bishop's dictum. "Ecclesiasticism in science is only unfaithfulness to truth."

Elijah's great question, "Will you serve God or Baal? Choose ye," is uttered audibly enough in the ears of every one of us as we come to manhood. Let every man who tries to answer it seriously, ask

* Charge at the Diocesan Synod of Brechin, "*Scotsman*," Sept. 14, 1871.

himself whether he can be satisfied with the Baal of authority, and with all the good things his worshippers are promised in this world and the next. If he can, let him, if he be so inclined, amuse himself with such scientific implements as authority tells him are safe and will not cut his fingers; but let him not imagine he is, or can be, both a true son of the Church and a loyal soldier of Science.

And, on the other hand, if the blind acceptance of authority appears to him in its true colours, as mere private judgment *in excelsis*, and if he have the courage to stand alone, face to face with the abyss of the Eternal and Unknowable, let him be content, once for all, not only to renounce the good things promised by " Infallibility," but even to bear the bad things which it prophesies; content to follow reason and fact in singleness and honesty of purpose, wherever they may lead, in the sure faith that a hell of honest men will, to him, be more endurable than a paradise full of angelic shams.

Mr. Mivart asserts that " without a belief in a personal God, there is no religion worthy of the name." This is a matter of opinion. But it may be asserted, with less reason to fear contradiction, that the worship of a personal God, who, on Mr. Mivart's hypothesis, must have used language studiously calculated to deceive his creatures and worshippers, is " no religion worthy of the name." " Incredibile est, Deum illis verbis ad populum fuisse locutum quibus deciperetur," is a verdict in which, for once, Jesuit casuistry concurs with the healthy moral sense of all mankind.

Having happily got quit of the theological aspect of evolution, the supporter of that great truth who turns to the scientific objections which are brought against it by recent criticism, finds, to his relief, that the work before him is greatly lightened by the spontaneous retreat of the enemy from nine-tenths of the territory which he occupied ten years ago. Even the Quarterly Reviewer not only abstains from venturing to deny that evolution has taken place, but he openly admits that Mr. Darwin has forced on men's minds " a recognition of the probability, if not more, of evolution, and of the certainty of the action of natural selection " (p. 49).

I do not quite see, myself, how, if the action of natural selection is *certain*, the occurrence of evolution is only *probable;* inasmuch as the development of a new species by natural selection is, so far as it goes, evolution. However, it is not worth while to quarrel with the precise terms of a sentence which shows that the high watermark of intelligence among those most respectable of Britons, the readers of the *Quarterly Review,* has now reached such a level, that the next tide may lift them easily and pleasantly on to the once-dreaded shore of evolution. Nor, having got there, do they seem likely to stop, until they have reached the inmost heart of that great region, and accepted the ape ancestry of, at any rate, the body of man. For the Reviewer admits that Mr. Darwin can be said to have established

" That if the various kinds of lower animals have been evolved one from the other by a process of natural generation or evolution, then, it becomes highly probable, *à priori*, that man's body has been similarly evolved ; but this, in such a case, becomes equally probable from the admitted fact that he is an animal at all " (p. 65).

From the principles laid down in the last sentence, it would follow that if man were constructed upon a plan as different from that of any other animal, as that of a sea-urchin is from that of a whale, it would be " equally probable " that he had been developed from some other animal, as it is now, when we know that for every bone, muscle, tooth, and even pattern of tooth, in man, there is a corresponding bone, muscle, tooth, and pattern of tooth, in an ape. And this shows one of two things—either that the Quarterly Reviewer's notions of probability are peculiar to himself ; or, that he has such an overpowering faith in the truth of evolution, that no extent of structural break between one animal and another is sufficient to destroy his conviction that evolution has taken place.

But this by the way. The importance of the admission that there is nothing in man's physical structure to interfere with his having been evolved from an ape, is not lessened, because it is grudgingly made and inconsistently qualified. And instead of jubilating over the extent of the enemy's retreat, it will be more worth while to lay siege to his last stronghold—the position that there is a distinction in kind between the mental faculties of man and those of brutes, and that, in consequence of this distinction in kind, no gradual progress from the mental faculties of the one to those of the other can have taken place.

The Quarterly Reviewer entrenches himself within formidable-looking psychological outworks, and there is no getting at him without attacking them one by one.

He begins by laying down the following proposition : " ' Sensation ' is not ' thought,' and no amount of the former would constitute the most rudimentary condition of the latter, though sensations supply the conditions for the existence of ' thought ' or ' knowledge ' " (p. 67).

This proposition is true, or not, according to the sense in which the word " thought " is employed. Thought is not uncommonly used in a sense co-extensive with consciousness, and, especially, with those states of consciousness we call memory. If I recall the impression made by a colour or an odour, and distinctly remember blueness or muskiness, I may say with perfect propriety that I "think of" blue or musk; and, so long as the thought lasts, it is simply a faint reproduction of the state of consciousness to which I gave the name in question, when it first became known to me as a sensation.

Now, if that faint reproduction of a sensation, which we call the memory of it, is properly termed a thought, it seems to me to be a somewhat forced proceeding to draw a hard and fast line of demarcation between thoughts and sensations. If sensations are not rudimentary thoughts, it may be said that some thoughts are rudimentary sensations. No amount of sound constitutes an echo, but for all that no one would pretend that an echo is something of totally different nature from a sound. Again, nothing can be looser, or more inaccurate, than the assertion that " sensations supply the conditions for the existence of thought or knowledge." If this implies that sensations supply the conditions for the existence of our memory of sensations, or of our thoughts about sensations, it is a truism which it is hardly worth while to state so solemnly. If it implies that sensations supply anything else it is obviously erroneous. And, if it means, as the context would seem to show it does, that sensations are the subject-matter of all thought or knowledge, then it is no less contrary to fact, inasmuch as our emotions, which constitute a large part of the subject-matter of thought or of knowledge, are not sensations.

More eccentric still is the Quarterly Reviewer's next piece of psychology.

" Altogether, we may clearly distinguish at least six kinds of action to which the nervous system ministers :—

" I. That in which impressions received result in appropriate movements without the intervention of sensation or thought, as in the cases of injury above given. (This is the reflex action of the nervous system.)

" II. That in which stimuli from without result in sensations through the agency of which their due effects are wrought out. (Sensation.)

" III. That in which impressions received result in sensations which give rise to the observation of sensible objects.—Sensible perception.

" IV. That in which sensations and perceptions continue to coalesce, agglutinate, and combine in more or less complex aggregations, according to the laws of the association of sensible perceptions.—Association.

" The above four groups contain only indeliberate operations, consisting, as they do at the best, but of mere *presentative* sensible ideas in no way implying any reflective or *representative* faculty. Such actions minister to and form *Instinct*. Besides these, we may distinguish two other kinds of mental action, namely :—

" V. That in which sensations and sensible perceptions are reflected on by thought and recognised as our own and we ourselves recognised by ourselves as affected and perceiving.—Self-consciousness.

" VI. That in which we reflect upon our sensations or perceptions, and ask what they are and why they are.—Reason.

" These two latter kinds of action are deliberate operations, performed, as they are, by means of representative ideas implying the use of a *reflective representative* faculty. Such actions distinguish the *intellect* or rational faculty. Now, we assert that possession in perfection of all the first four (*presentative*) kinds of action by no means implies the possession of the last two (*representative*) kinds. All persons, we think, must admit the truth of the following proposition :—

"Two faculties are distinct, not in degree but *in kind*, if we may possess the one in perfection without that fact implying that we possess the other also. Still more will this be the case if the two faculties tend to increase in an inverse ratio. Yet this is the distinction between the *instinctive* and the *intellectual* parts of man's nature.

"As to animals, we fully admit that they may possess all the first four groups of actions—that they may have, so to speak, mental images of sensible objects combined in all degrees of complexity, as governed by the laws of association. We deny to them, on the other hand, the possession of the last two kinds of mental action. We deny them, that is, the power of reflecting on their own existence or of enquiring into the nature of objects and their causes. We deny that they know that they know or know themselves in knowing. In other words, we deny them *reason*. The possession of the presentative faculty, as above explained, in no way implies that of the reflective faculty; nor does any amount of direct operation imply the power of asking the reflective question before mentioned, as to 'what' and 'why.'" (*l. c.* p. 67-8.)

Sundry points are worthy of notice in this remarkable account of the intellectual powers. In the first place, the Reviewer ignores emotion and volition, though they are no inconsiderable "kinds of action to which the nervous system ministers," and memory has a place in his classification only by implication. Secondly, we are told that the second "kind of action to which the nervous system ministers" is "that in which stimuli from without result in sensations through the agency of which their due effects are wrought out. (Sensation.)" Does this really mean that, in the writer's opinion, "sensation" is the "agent" by which the "due effect" of the stimulus, which gives rise to sensation, is "wrought out?" Suppose somebody runs a pin into me. The "due effect" of that particular stimulus will probably be threefold; namely, a sensation of pain, a start, and an interjectional expletive. Does the Quarterly Reviewer really think that the "sensation" is the "agent" by which the other two phenomena are wrought out?

But these matters are of little moment to any one but the Reviewer and those persons who may incautiously take their physiology, or psychology, from him. The really interesting point is this, that when he fully admits that animals "may possess all the first four groups of actions," he grants all that is necessary for the purposes of the evolutionist. For he hereby admits that in animals "impressions received result in sensations which give rise to the observation of sensible objects," and that they have what he calls "sensible perception." Nor was it possible to help the admission; for we have as much reason to ascribe to animals, as we have to attribute to our fellow-men, the power, not only of perceiving external objects, as external, and thus practically recognising the difference between the self and the not-self; but that of distinguishing between like and unlike, and between simultaneous and successive things. When a gamekeeper goes out coursing with a greyhound in leash, and a hare crosses the field of vision, he becomes the subject of those states of consciousness we call visual sensations, and that is all he receives from without. Sensation, as such, tells him nothing whatever about the cause of these states of consciousness; but the thinking faculty instantly goes to work upon the raw material of sensation furnished to it through the eye, and gives rise to a train of thoughts. First comes the thought that there is an object at a certain distance; then arises another thought—the perception of the likeness between the states of consciousness awakened by this object to those presented by memory, as, on some former occasion, called up by a hare; this is succeeded by another thought of the nature of an emotion— namely, the desire to possess a hare; then follows a longer or shorter train of other thoughts, which end in a volition and an act—the loosing of the greyhound from the leash. These several thoughts are the concomitants of a process which goes on in the nervous system of the man. Unless the nerve-elements of the retina, of the optic nerve, of the brain, of the spinal chord, and of the nerves of the arms went through certain physical changes in due order and correlation, the various states of consciousness which have been enumerated would not make their appearance. So that in this, as in all other intellectual operations, we have to distinguish two sets of successive changes—one in the physical basis of consciousness, and the other in consciousness itself; one set which may, and doubtless will, in course of time, be followed through all their complexities by the anatomist and the physicist, and one of which only the man himself can have immediate knowledge.

As it is very necessary to keep up a clear distinction between these two processes, let the one be called *neurosis*, and the other *psychosis*. When the gamekeeper was first trained to his work, every step in the process of neurosis was accompanied by a corresponding step in that of psychosis, or nearly so. He was conscious of seeing something, conscious of making sure it was a hare, conscious of desiring to catch it, and therefore to loose the greyhound at the right time, conscious of the acts by which he let the dog out of the leash. But with practice, though the various steps of the neurosis remain—for otherwise the impression on the retina would not result in the loosing of the dog—the great majority of the steps of the psychosis vanish, and the loosing of the dog follows unconsciously, or as we say, without thinking about it, upon the sight of the hare. No one will deny that the series of acts which originally intervened between the sensation and the letting go of the dog were, in the strictest sense, intellectual and rational operations. Do they cease to be so when the man ceases to be conscious of them? That depends upon what is the essence and what the accident of those operations, which, taken together, constitute ratiocination.

Now ratiocination is resolvable into predication, and predication consists in marking, in some way, the existence, the coexistence, the succession, the likeness and unlikeness, of things or their ideas. Whatever does this reasons; and if a machine produces the effects of reason, I see no more ground for denying to it the reasoning power, because it is unconscious, than I see for refusing to Mr. Babbage's engine the title of a calculating machine on the same grounds.

Thus it seems to me that a gamekeeper reasons, whether he is conscious or unconscious, whether his reasoning is carried on by neurosis alone, or whether it involves more or less psychosis. And if this is true of the gamekeeper, it is also true of the greyhound. The essential resemblances in all points of structure and function, so far as they can be studied, between the nervous systems of the man and that of the dog, leave no reasonable doubt that the processes which go on in the one are just like those which take place in the other. In the dog, there can be no doubt that the nervous matter which lies between the retina and the muscles undergoes a series of changes, precisely analogous to those which, in the man, give rise to sensation, a train of thought, and volition.

Whether this neurosis is accompanied by such psychosis as ours, it is impossible to say; but those who deny that the nervous changes, which, in the dog, correspond with those which underlie thought in a man, are accompanied by consciousness, are equally bound to maintain that those nervous changes in the dog, which correspond with those which underlie sensation in a man, are also unaccompanied by consciousness. In other words, if there is no ground for believing that a dog thinks, neither is there any for believing that he feels.

As is well known, Descartes boldly faced this dilemma, and maintained that all animals were mere machines and entirely devoid of consciousness. But he did not deny, nor can any one deny, that in this case they are reasoning machines, capable of performing all those operations which are performed by the nervous system of man when he reasons. For even supposing that in man, and in man only, psychosis is superadded to neurosis—the neurosis which is common to both man and animal gives their reasoning processes a fundamental unity. But Descartes's position is open to very serious objections, if the evidence that animals feel is insufficient to prove that they really do so. What is the value of the evidence which leads one to believe that one's fellow-man feels? The only evidence in this argument of analogy, is the similarity of his structure and of his actions to one's own. And if that is good enough to prove that one's fellow-man feels, surely it is good enough to prove that an ape feels. For the differences of structure and function between men and apes are utterly insufficient to warrant the assumption, that while men have those states of consciousness we call sensations, apes have nothing of the kind. Moreover, we have as good evidence that apes are capable of emotion and volition as we have that men other than ourselves are. But if apes possess three out of the four kinds of states of consciousness which we discover in ourselves, what possible reason is there for denying them the fourth? If they are capable of sensation, emotion, and volition, why are they to be denied thought (in the sense of predication)?

No answer has ever been given to these questions. And as the law of continuity is as much opposed, as is the common sense of mankind, to the notion that all animals are unconscious machines, it may safely be assumed that no sufficient answer ever will be given to them.

There is every reason to believe that consciousness is a function of nervous matter, when that nervous matter has attained a certain degree of organization, just as we know the other "actions to which the nervous system ministers," such as reflex action and the like, to be. As I have ventured to state my view of the matter elsewhere, " our thoughts are the expression of molecular changes in that matter of life which is the source of our other vital phenomena."

Mr. Wallace objects to this statement in the following terms:—

"Not having been able to find any clue in Professor Huxley's writings, to the steps by which he passes from those vital phenomena, which consist only, in their last analysis, of movements by particles of matter, to those other phenomena which we term thought, sensation, or consciousness; but, knowing that so positive an expression of opinion from him will have great weight with many persons, I shall endeavour to show, with as much brevity as is compatible with clearness, that this theory is not only incapable of proof, but is also, as it appears to me, inconsistent with accurate conceptions of molecular physics."

With all respect for Mr. Wallace, it appears to me that his remarks are entirely beside the question. I really know nothing whatever, and never hope to know anything, of the steps by which the passage from molecular movement to states of consciousness is effected; and I entirely agree with the sense of the passage 'which he quotes from Professor Tyndall, apparently imagining that it is in opposition to the view I hold.

All that I have to say is, that, in my belief, consciousness and molecular action are capable of being expressed by one another, just as heat and mechanical action are capable of being expressed in terms of one another. Whether we shall ever be able to express consciousness in foot-pounds, or not, is more than I will venture to say; but that there is evidence of the existence of some correlation between mechanical motion and consciousness is as plain as anything can be. Suppose the poles of an electric battery to be connected by a platinum wire. A certain intensity of the current gives rise in the mind of a bystander to that state of consciousness we call a " dull red light "—a little greater intensity to another which we call a " bright red light; " increase the intensity, and the light becomes white; and, finally, it dazzles, and a new state of consciousness arises, which we term pain. Given the same wire and the same nervous apparatus, and the amount of electric force required to give rise to these several states of consciousness will be the same, however often the experiment is repeated. And as the electric force, the light-waves, and the nerve-vibrations caused by the impact of the light-waves on the retina, are all expressions of the molecular changes which are taking place in the elements of the battery ; so consciousness is, in the same sense, an expression of the molecular changes which take place in that nervous matter, which is the organ of consciousness.

And, since this, and any number of similar examples that may be required, prove that one form of consciousness, at any rate, is, in the strictest sense, the expression of molecular change, it really is not worth while to pursue the inquiry, whether a fact so easily established is consistent with any particular system of molecular physics or not.

Mr. Wallace, in fact, appears to me to have mixed up two very distinct propositions : the one, the indisputable truth that consciousness is correlated with molecular changes in the organ of consciousness ; the other, that the nature of that correlation is known, or can be conceived, which is quite another matter. Mr. Wallace presumably believes in that correlation of phenomena which we call cause and effect as firmly as I do. But if he has ever been able to form the faintest notion how a cause gives rise to its effect, all I can say is that I envy him. Take the simplest case imaginable—suppose a ball in motion to impinge upon another ball at rest. I know very well, as a matter of fact, that the ball in motion will communicate some of its motion to the ball at rest, and that the motion of the two balls after collision is precisely correlated with the masses of both balls and the amount of motion of the first. But how does this come about ? In what manner can we conceive that the *vis viva* of the first ball passes into the second? I confess I can no more form any conception of what happens in this case, than I can of what takes place when the motion of particles of my nervous matter, caused by the impact of a similar ball, gives rise to the state of consciousness I call pain. In ultimate analysis everything is incomprehensible, and the whole object of science is simply to reduce the fundamental incomprehensibilities to the smallest possible number.

But to return to the Quarterly Reviewer. He admits that animals have "mental images of sensible objects, combined in all degrees of complexity, as governed by the laws of association." Presumably, by this confused and imperfect statement the Reviewer means to admit more than the words imply. For mental images of sensible objects, even though "combined in all degrees of complexity," are, and can be, nothing more than mental images of sensible objects. But judgments, emotions, and volitions cannot by any possibility be included under the head of "mental images of sensible objects." If the greyhound had no better mental endowment than the Reviewer allows him, he might have the "mental image" of the "sensible object"—the hare—and that might be combined with the mental images of other sensible objects, to any degree of complexity, but he would have no power of judging it to be at a certain distance from him; no power of perceiving its similarity to his memory of a hare; and no desire to get at it. Consequently he would stand stock still, and the noble art of coursing would have no existence. On the other hand, as that art is largely practised, it follows that greyhounds alone possess a number of mental powers, the existence of which, in any animal, is absolutely denied by the Quarterly Reviewer.

Finally, what are the mental powers which he reserves as the especial prerogative of man? They are two. First, the recognition of "ourselves by ourselves as affected and perceiving. Self-consciousness"

Secondly. "The reflection upon our sensations and perceptions, and asking what they are and why they are. Reason."

To the faculty defined in the last sentence, the Reviewer, without assigning the least ground for thus departing from both common usage and technical propriety, applies the name of reason. But if man is not to be considered a reasoning being, unless he asks what his sensations and perceptions are and why they are, what is a Hottentot, an Australian black fellow, or what the "swinked hedger" of an ordinary agricultural district? Nay, what becomes of an average country squire or parson? How many of these worthy persons who, as their wont is, read the *Quarterly Review,* would do other than stand agape, if you asked him whether he had ever reflected what his sensations and perceptions are, and why they are?

So that if the Reviewer's new definition of reason be correct, the majority of men, even among the most civilised nations, are devoid of that supreme characteristic of manhood. And if it be as absurd as I believe it to be, then, as reason is certainly not self-consciousness, and as it, as certainly, is one of the "actions to which the nervous system ministers," we must, if the Reviewer's classification is to be adopted, seek it among those four faculties which he allows animals to possess. And thus, for the second time, he really surrenders, while seeming to defend, his position.

The Quarterly Reviewer, as we have seen, lectures the evolutionists upon their want of knowledge of philosophy altogether. Mr. Mivart is not less pained at Mr. Darwin's ignorance of moral science. It is grievous to him that Mr. Darwin (and *nous autres*) should not have grasped the elementary distinction between material and formal morality; and he lays down as an axiom, of which no tyro ought to be ignorant, the position that "Acts, unaccompanied by mental acts of·conscious will directed towards the fulfilment of duty," are "absolutely destitute of the most incipient degree of real or formal goodness."

Now this may be Mr. Mivart's opinion, but it is a proposition which, really, does not stand on the footing of an undisputed axiom. Mr. Mill denies it in his work on Utilitarianism. The most influential writer of a totally opposed school, Mr. Carlyle, is never weary of denying it, and upholding the merit of that virtue which is unconscious; nay, it is, to my understanding, extremely hard to reconcile Mr. Mivart's dictum with that noble summary of the whole duty of man—"Thou shalt love the Lord thy God with all thy heart, and with all thy soul, and with all thy strength: and thou shalt love thy neighbour as thy self." According to Mr. Mivart's definition, the man who loves God and his neighbour, and out of sheer love and affection for both, does all he can to please them, is, nevertheless, destitute of a particle of real goodness.

And it further happens that Mr. Darwin, who is charged by Mr. Mivart with being ignorant of the distinction between material and formal goodness, discusses the very question at issue, in a passage which is well worth reading (vol. i. p. 87), and also comes to a conclusion opposed to Mr. Mivart's axiom. A proposition which has been so much disputed and repudiated, should, under no circumstances, have been thus confidently assumed to be true. For myself, I utterly reject it, inasmuch as the logical consequence of the adoption of any such principle is the denial of all moral value to sympathy and affection. According to Mr. Mivart's axiom, the man who, seeing another struggling in the water, leaps in at the risk of his own life to save him, does that which is "destitute of the most incipient degree of real goodness," unless, as he strips off his coat, he says to himself, "Now mind, I am going to do this because it is my duty and for no other reason;" and the most beautiful character to which humanity can attain, that of the man who does good without thinking about it, because he loves justice and mercy and is repelled by evil, has no claim on our moral approbation. The denial that a man acts morally because he does not think whether he does so or not, may be put upon the same footing as the denial of the title of an arithmetician to the calculating boy, because he did not know how he worked his sums. If mankind ever generally accept and act upon Mr. Mivart's axiom, they will simply become a set of most unendurable prigs; but they never have accepted it, and I venture to hope that evolution has nothing so terrible in store for the human race.

But, if an action, the motive of which is nothing but affection or sympathy, may be deserving of moral approbation and really good, who that has ever had a dog of his own will deny that animals are capable of such actions? Mr. Mivart indeed says:—"It may be safely affirmed, however, that there is no trace in brutes of any actions simulating morality which are not explicable by the fear of punishment, by the hope of pleasure, or by personal affection" (p. 221). But it may be affirmed, with equal truth, that there is no trace in men of any actions which are not traceable to the same motives. If a man does anything, he does it either because he fears to be punished if he does not do it, or because he hopes to obtain pleasure by doing it, or because he gratifies his affections * by doing it.

Assuming the position of the absolute moralists, let it be granted that there is a perception of right and wrong innate in every man. This means, simply, that when certain ideas are presented to his mind, the feeling of approbation arises, and when certain others, the feeling of disapprobation. To do your duty is to earn the approbation of your conscience, or moral sense; to fail in your duty is to feel its disapprobation, as we all say. Now, is approbation a pleasure or a pain? Surely a pleasure. And is disapprobation a pleasure or a pain? Surely a pain. Consequently all that is really meant by the absolute moralists is that there is, in the very nature of man, something which enables him to be conscious of these particular pleasures and pains. And when they talk of immutable and eternal principles of morality, the only intelligible sense which I can put upon the words, is that the nature of man being what it is, he always has been

---

* In separating pleasure and the gratification of affection, I simply follow Mr. Mivart without admitting the justice of the separation.

and always will be capable of feeling these particular pleasures and pains. *A priori*, I have nothing to say against this proposition. Admitting its truth, I do not see how the moral faculty is on a different footing from any of the other faculties of man. If I choose to say that it is an immutable and eternal law of human nature that "ginger is hot in the mouth" the assertion has as much foundation of truth as the other, though I think it would be expressed in needlessly pompous language. I must confess that I have never been able to understand why there should be such a bitter quarrel between the intuitionists and the utilitarians. The intuitionist is after all only a utilitarian who believes that a particular class of pleasures and pains has an especial importance, by reason of its foundation in the nature of man, and its inseparable connection with his very existence as a thinking being. And as regards the motive of personal affection: Love, as Spinoza profoundly says, is the association of pleasure with that which is loved.* Or, to put it to the common sense of mankind, is the gratification of affection a pleasure or a pain? Surely a pleasure. So that whether the motive which leads us to perform an action is the love of our neighbour, or the love of God, it is undeniable that pleasure enters into that motive.

Thus much in reply to Mr. Mivart's arguments. I cannot but think that it is to be regretted that he ekes them out by ascribing to the doctrines of the philosophers, with whom he does not agree, logical consequences which have been over and over again proved not to flow from them; and when reason fails him, tries the effect of an injurious nickname. According to the views of Mr. Spencer, Mr. Mill, and Mr. Darwin, Mr. Mivart tells us, "*virtue is a mere kind of retrieving ;*" and, that we may not miss the point of the joke, he puts it in italics. But what if it is? Does that make it less virtue? Suppose I say that sculpture is a "mere way" of stone-cutting, and painting a "mere way" of daubing canvas, and music a "mere way" of making a noise, the statements are quite true; but they only show that I see no other method of depreciating some of the noblest aspects of humanity, than that of using language in an inadequate and misleading sense about them. And the peculiar inappropriateness of this particular nickname to the views in question, arises from the circumstance which Mr. Mivart would doubtless have recollected, if his wish to ridicule had not for the moment obscured his judgment—that whether the law of evolution applies to man or not, that of hereditary transmission certainly does. Mr. Mivart will hardly deny that a man owes a large share of the moral tendencies which he exhibits to his ancestors; and the man who inherits a desire to steal from a kleptomaniac, or

* "Nempe, Amor nihil aliud est, quam Lœtitia, concomitante idea causœ externœ." —*Ethices*, III. xiii.

a tendency to benevolence from a Howard, is, so far as he illustrates hereditary transmission, comparable to the dog who inherits the desire to fetch a duck out of the water from his retrieving sire. So that, evolution, or no evolution, moral qualities are comparable to a "kind of retrieving;" though the comparison, if meant for the purposes of casting obloquy on evolution, does not say much for the fairness of those who make it.

The Quarterly Reviewer and Mr. Mivart base their objections to the evolution of the mental faculties of man from those of some lower animal form, upon what they maintain to be a difference in kind between the mental and moral faculties of men and brutes; and I have endeavoured to show, by exposing the utter unsoundness of their philosophical basis, that these objections are devoid of importance.

The objections which Mr. Wallace brings forward to the doctrine of the evolution of the mental faculties of man from those of brutes by natural causes, are of a different order, and require separate consideration.

If I understand him rightly, he by no means doubts that both the bodily and the mental faculties of man have been evolved from those of some lower animal; but he is of opinion, that some agency beyond that which has been concerned in the evolution of ordinary animals, has been operative in the case of man. "A superior intelligence has guided the development of man in a definite direction and for a special purpose, just as man guides the development of many animal and vegetable forms."* I understand this to mean that, just as the rock-pigeon has been produced by natural causes, while the evolution of the tumbler from the blue rock has required the special inter- vention of the intelligence of man, so some anthropoid form may have been evolved by variation and natural selection, but it could never have given rise to man, unless some superior intelligence had played the part of the pigeon-fancier.

According to Mr. Wallace, "whether we compare the savage with the higher developments of man, or with the brutes around him, we are alike driven to the conclusion, that, in his large and well- developed brain he possesses an organ quite disproportioned to his requirements" (p. 343); and he asks, "What is there in the life of the savage but the satisfying of the cravings of appetite in the simplest and easiest way? What thoughts, ideas, or actions are there that raise him many grades above the elephant or the ape?" (p. 342). I answer Mr. Wallace by citing a remarkable passage which occurs in his instructive paper on " Instinct in Man and Animals."

" Savages make long journeys in many directions, and, their whole

* "The limits of Natural Selection as applied to Man " (*l. c.* p. 359).

faculties being directed to the subject, they gain a wide and accurate knowledge of the topography, not only of their own district, but of all the regions round about. Every one who has travelled in a new direction communicates his knowledge to those who have travelled less, and descriptions of routes and localities, and minute incidents of travel, form one of the main staples of conversation around the evening fire. Every wanderer or captive from another tribe adds to the store of information, and, as the very existence of individuals and of whole families and tribes depends upon the completeness of this knowledge, all the acute perceptive faculties of the adult savage are directed to acquiring and perfecting it. The good hunter or warrior thus comes to know the bearing of every hill and mountain range, the directions and junctions of all the streams, the situation of each tract characterized by peculiar vegetation, not only within the area he has himself traversed, but perhaps for a hundred miles around it. His acute observation enables him to detect the slightest undulations of the surface, the various changes of subsoil and alterations in the character of the vegetation that would be quite imperceptible to a stranger. His eye is always open to the direction in which he is going ; the mossy side of trees, the presence of certain plants under the shade of rocks, the morning and evening flight of birds, are to him indications of direction almost as sure as the sun in the heavens " (pp. 207-8).

I have seen enough of savages to be able to declare that nothing can be more admirable than this description of what a savage has to learn. But it is incomplete. Add to all this the knowledge which a savage is obliged to gain of the properties of plants, of the characters and habits of animals, and of the minute indications by which their course is discoverable ; consider that even an Australian can make excellent baskets and nets, and neatly fitted and beautifully balanced spears ; that he learns to use these so as to be able to transfix a quartern loaf at sixty yards ; and that very often, as in the case of the American Indians, the language of a savage exhibits complexities which a well-trained European finds it difficult to master ; consider that every time a savage tracks his game, he employs a minuteness of observation, and an accuracy of inductive and deductive reasoning which, applied to other matters, would assure some reputation to a man of science, and I think we need ask no further why he possesses such a fair supply of brains. In complexity and difficulty, I should say that the intellectual labour of a " good hunter or warrior" considerably exceeds that of an ordinary Englishman. The Civil Service Examiners are held in great terror by young Englishmen ; but even their ferocity never tempted them to require a candidate to possess such a knowledge of a parish, as Mr. Wallace justly points out savages may possess of an area a hundred miles, or more, in diameter.

But suppose, for the sake of argument, that a savage has more brains than seems proportioned to his wants, all that can be said is that the objection to natural selection, if it be one, applies quite as strongly to the lower animals. The brain of a porpoise is quite wonderful for its mass, and for the development of the cerebral convolutions. And yet since we have ceased to credit the story of Arion, it is hard to believe that porpoises are much troubled with intellect; and still more difficult is it to imagine that their big brains are only a preparation for the advent of some accomplished cetacean of the future. Surely, again, a wolf must have too much brains, or else how is it that a dog, with only the same quantity and form of brain, is able to develop such singular intelligence? The wolf stands to the dog in the same relation as the savage to the man; and, therefore, if Mr. Wallace's doctrine holds good, some higher power must have superintended the breeding up of wolves from some inferior stock, in order to prepare them to become dogs.

Mr. Wallace further maintains that the origin of some of man's mental faculties by the preservation of useful variations is not possible. Such, for example, are " the capacity to form ideal conceptions of space and time, of eternity and infinity; the capacity for intense artistic feelings of pleasure in form, colour, and composition; and for those abstract notions of form and number which render geometry and arithmetic possible." " How," he asks, " were all or any of these faculties first developed, when they could have been of no possible use to man in his early stages of barbarism ? "

Surely the answer is not far to seek. *The* lowest savages are as devoid of any such conceptions as the brutes themselves. What sort of conceptions of space and time, of form and number, can be possessed by a savage who has not got so far as to be able to count beyond five or six, who does not know how to draw a triangle or. a circle, and has not the remotest notion of separating the particular quality we call form, from the other qualities of bodies? None of these capacities are exhibited by men, unless they form part of a tolerably advanced society. And, in such a society, there are abundant conditions by which a selective influence is exerted in favour of those persons who exhibit an approximation towards the possession of these capacities.

The savage who can amuse his fellows by telling a good story over the nightly fire, is held by them in esteem and rewarded, in one way or another, for so doing—in other words, it is an advantage to him to possess this power. He who can carve a paddle, or the figurehead of a canoe better, similarly profits beyond his duller neighbour. He who counts a little better than others, gets most yams when barter is going on, and forms the shrewdest estimate of the numbers of an opposing tribe. *The* experience of daily life shows that the conditions of our present social existence exercise the most extraordinarily powerful selective influence in favour of novelists, artists, and strong intellects of all kinds; and it seems unquestionable that all forms of social existence must have had the same tendency, if we consider the indisputable facts that even animals possess the power of distinguishing form and number, and that they are capable of deriving pleasure from particular forms and sounds. If we admit, as Mr. Wallace does, that the lowest savages are not raised " many grades above the elephant and the ape ;" and if we further admit, as I contend must be admitted, that the conditions of social life tend, powerfully, to give an advantage to those individuals who vary in the direction of intellectual or æsthetic excellence, what is there to interfere with the belief that these higher faculties, like the rest, owe their development to natural selection ?

Finally, with respect to the development of the moral sense out of the simple feelings of pleasure and pain, liking and disliking, with which the lower animals are provided, I can find nothing in Mr. Wallace's reasonings which has not already been met by Mr. Mill, Mr. Spencer, or Mr. Darwin.

I do not propose to follow the Quarterly Reviewer and Mr. Mivart through the long string of objections in matters of detail which they bring against Mr. Darwin's views. Every one who has considered the matter carefully will be able to ferret out as many more " difficulties ;" but he will also, I believe, fail as completely as they appear to me to have done, in bringing forward any fact which is really contradictory of Mr. Darwin's views. Occasionally, too, their objections and criticisms are based upon errors of their own. As, for example, when Mr. Mivart and the Quarterly Reviewer insist upon the resemblances between the eyes of *Cephalopoda* and *Vertebrata*, quite forgetting that there are striking and altogether fundamental differences between them ; or when the Quarterly Reviewer corrects Mr. Darwin for saying that the gibbons, "without having been taught, can walk or run upright with tolerable quickness, though they move awkwardly, and much less securely than man."

The Quarterly Reviewer says, " This is a little misleading, inasmuch as it is not stated that this upright progression is effected by placing the enormously long arms behind the head, or holding them out backwards as a balance in progression."

Now, before carping at a small statement like this, the Quarterly Reviewer should have made sure that he was quite right. But he happens to be quite wrong. I suspect he got his notion of the manner in which a gibbon walks from a citation in "Man's Place in Nature." But at that time I had not seen a gibbon walk. Since then I have, and I can testify that nothing can be more precise than Mr. Darwin's statement. The gibbon I saw walked without either putting his arms behind his head or holding them out backwards. All he did was to touch the ground with the outstretched fingers of his long arms now and then, just as one sees a man who carries a stick, but does not need one, touch the ground with it as he walks along.

Again, a large number of the objections brought forward by Mr. Mivart and the Quarterly Reviewer apply to evolution in general, quite as much as to the particular form of that doctrine advocated by Mr. Darwin ; or, to their notions of Mr. Darwin's views and not to what they really are. An excellent example of this class of difficulties is to be found in Mr. Mivart's chapter on "Independent similarities of structure." Mr. Mivart says that these cannot be explained by an "absolute and pure Darwinian," but "that an innate power and evolutionary law, aided by the corrective action of natural selection, should have furnished like needs with like aids, is not at all improbable " (p. 82).

I do not exactly know what Mr. Mivart means by an "absolute and pure Darwinian ;" indeed Mr. Mivart makes that creature hold so many singular opinions that I doubt if I can ever have seen one alive. But I find nothing in his statement of the view which he imagines to be originated by himself, which is really inconsistent with what I understand to be Mr. Darwin's views.

I apprehend that the foundation of the theory of natural selection is the fact that living bodies tend incessantly to vary. This variation is neither indefinite, nor fortuitous, nor does it take place in all directions, in the strict sense of these words.

Accurately speaking, it is not indefinite, nor does it take place in all directions, because it is limited by the general characters of the type to which the organism exhibiting the variation belongs. A whale does not tend to vary in the direction of producing feathers, nor a bird in the direction of developing whalebone. In popular language there is no harm in saying that the waves which break upon the seashore are indefinite, fortuitous, and break in all directions. In scientific language, on the contrary, such a statement would be a gross error, inasmuch as every particle of foam is the result of perfectly definite forces, operating according to no less definite laws. In like manner, every variation of a living form, however minute, however apparently accidental, is inconceivable except as the expression of the operation of molecular forces or "powers " resident within the organism. And, as these forces certainly operate according to definite laws, their general result is, doubtless, in accordance with some general law which subsumes them all. And there appears to be no objection to call this an "evolutionary law." But nobody is the wiser for doing so, or has thereby contributed, in the least degree, to the advance of the doctrine of evolution, the great need of which is a theory of variation.

When Mr. Mivart tells us that his "aim has been to support the doctrine that these species have been evolved by ordinary *natural laws* (for the most part unknown) aided by the *subordinate* action of 'natural selection' " (p. 332-3), he seems to be of opinion that his enterprise has the merit of novelty. All I can say is that I have never had the slightest notion that Mr. Darwin's aim is in any way different from this. If I affirm that "species have been evolved by variation * (a natural process, the laws of which are for the most part unknown), aided by the subordinate action of natural selection," it seems to me that I enunciate a proposition which constitutes the very pith and marrow of the first edition of the " Origin of Species." And what the evolutionist stands in need of just now, is not an iteration of the fundamental principle of Darwinism, but some light upon the questions, What are the limits of variation ? and, If a variety has arisen, can that variety be perpetuated, or even intensified, when selective conditions are indifferent, or perhaps unfavourable, to its existence ? I cannot find that Mr. Darwin has ever been very dogmatic in answering these questions. Formerly, he seems to have inclined to reply to them in the negative, while now his inclination is the other way. Leaving aside those broad questions of theology, philosophy, and ethics, by the discussion of which neither the Quarterly Reviewer nor Mr. Mivart can be said to have damaged Darwinism—whatever else they have injured—this is what their criticisms come to. They confound a struggle for some rifle-pits with an assault on the fortress.

In some respects, finally, I can only characterize the Quarterly Reviewer's treatment of Mr. Darwin as alike unjust and unbecoming. Language of this strength requires justification, and on that ground I add the remarks which follow.

The Quarterly Reviewer opens his essay by a careful enumeration of all these points upon which, during the course of thirteen years of incessant labour, Mr. Darwin has modified his opinions. It has often and justly been remarked, that what strikes a candid student of Mr. Darwin's works is not so much his industry, his knowledge, or even the surprising fertility of his inventive genius; but that unswerving truthfulness and honesty which never permit him to hide a weak place, or gloss over a difficulty, but lead him, on all occasions, to point out the weak places in his own armour, and even sometimes, it appears to me, to make admissions against himself which are quite unneccessary. A critic who desires to attack Mr. Darwin has only to read his works with a desire to observe, not their merits, but their defects, and he will find, ready to hand, more adverse suggestions, than are likely ever to have suggested themselves to his own sharpness without Mr. Darwin's self-denying aid.

Now this quality of scientific candour is not so common that it needs to be discouraged; and it appears to me to deserve other treatment than that adopted by the Quarterly Reviewer, who deals

* Including under this head hereditary transmission.

with Mr. Darwin as an Old Bailey barrister deals with a man against whom he wishes to obtain a conviction, *per fas aut nefas*, and opens his case by endeavouring to create a prejudice against the prisoner in the mind of the jury. In his eagerness to carry out this laudable design, the Quarterly Reviewer cannot even state the history of the doctrine of natural selection without an oblique and entirely unjustifiable attempt to depreciate Mr. Darwin. "*To* Mr. Darwin," says he, "and (through Mr. Wallace's reticence) to Mr. Darwin alone, is due the credit of having first brought it prominently forward and demonstrated its truth." No one can less desire than I do, to throw a doubt upon Mr. Wallace's originality, or to question his claim to the honour of being one of the originators of the doctrine of natural selection; but the statement that Mr. Darwin has the sole credit of originating the doctrine because of Mr. Wallace's reticence is simply ridiculous. The proof of this is, in the first place, afforded by Mr. Wallace himself, whose noble freedom from petty jealousy in this matter, smaller folk would do well to imitate; and who writes thus:—"I have felt all my life, and I still feel, the most sincere satisfaction that Mr. Darwin had been at work long before me, and that it was not left for me to attempt to write the 'Origin of Species.' I have long since measured my own strength, and know well that it would be quite unequal to that task." So that if there was any reticence at all in the matter, it was Mr. Darwin's reticence during the long twenty years of study which intervened between the conception and the publication of his theory, which gave Mr. Wallace the chance of being an independent discoverer of the importance of natural selection. And, finally, if it be recollected that Mr. Darwin's and Mr. Wallace's essays were published simultaneously in the *Journal of the Linnæan Society* for 1858, it follows that the Reviewer, while obliquely depreciating Mr. Darwin's deserts, has, in reality, awarded to him a priority which, in legal strictness, does not exist.

Mr. Mivart, whose opinions so often concur with those of the Quarterly Reviewer, puts the case in a way, which I much regret to be obliged to say, is, in my judgment, quite as incorrect; though the injustice may be less glaring. He says that the theory of natural selection is, in general, exclusively associated with the name of Mr. Darwin, "on account of the noble self-abnegation of Mr. Wallace." As I have said, no one can honour Mr. Wallace more than I do, both for what he has done and for what he has not done, in his relation to Mr. Darwin. And perhaps nothing is more creditable to him than his frank declaration that he could not have written such a work as the "Origin of Species." But, by this declaration, the person most directly interested in the matter repudiates, by anticipation, Mr. Mivart's suggestion that Mr. Darwin's eminence is more or less due to Mr. Wallace's modesty.   T. H. HUXLEY.

ON THE USE OF THE WORD PERSON IN LATIN THEOLOGY.

"In rationali natura esse *aliud* et *aliud* fecit diversitas substantiarum, esse *alium* et esse *alium* facit alietas personarum."—*Richard de S. Victor. De Trinitate*, lib. iv. c. 6.

"Pluralitas substantiarum non facit *alium* et *alium* in humana natura, nec pluralitas personarum facit *aliud* et *aliud* in natura divina."—*Ibid.*, c. 10.

THE questions that have clustered round the document commonly called the Athanasian Creed are numerous and distinct. Ought it to be retained as an authorized formulary of the Church at all? If so retained, ought it to form part of our public services, or be relegated to a position like that of the Articles? If it is to continue being said or sung in the service, ought it to be retranslated? Is it objectionable, either in itself or as translated, by reason of what are called the damnatory clauses, or the dogmatic statements, or both? Here are several issues, on which contending parties might easily be seen in the most varying relative positions. My concern at present, however, has but little reference to these. I wish merely to vindicate a single word, the use of which has been attacked by a recent distinguished advocate of retranslation. My aim is not confined to the Athanasian Creed; for the word *Person*, which is that in question, is used elsewhere in the Prayer-Book and in the Articles, is doubtless largely employed in catechetical and private explanation, and by our Presbyterian and Dissenting brethren as well as ourselves. In short, its retention or abandonment is a question which concerns the whole Western Church.

CPSIA information can be obtained
at www.ICGtesting.com
Printed in the USA
BVHW03s0501170518
516410BV00025B/687/P